Dangerous
SPIDERS
AN IMAGINATION LIBRARY SERIES

Hobo
S P I D E R S

by Eric Ethan

Gareth Stevens Publishing
A WORLD ALMANAC EDUCATION GROUP COMPANY

Please visit our web site at: www.garethstevens.com
For a free color catalog describing Gareth Stevens Publishing's
list of high-quality books and multimedia programs,
call 1-800-542-2595 (USA) or 1-800-387-3178 (Canada).
Gareth Stevens Publishing's fax: (414) 332-3567.

Library of Congress Cataloging-in-Publication Data

Ethan, Eric.
    Hobo spiders / by Eric Ethan.
      p. cm. — (Dangerous spiders—an imagination library series)
    Summary: An introduction to the physical characteristics, behavior, and life cycle
of hobo spiders, also known as aggressive house spiders.
    Includes bibliographical references and index.
    ISBN 0-8368-3768-1 (lib. bdg.)
    1. Hobo spider—Juvenile literature. [1. Hobo spider. 2. Spiders.] I. Title.
QL458.42.A3E84   2003
595.4'4—dc21   2003045554

First published in 2004 by
Gareth Stevens Publishing
A World Almanac Education Group Company
330 West Olive Street, Suite 100
Milwaukee, WI 53212 USA

Text: Eric Ethan
Cover design and page layout: Scott M. Krall
Text editor: Susan Ashley
Series editor: Dorothy L. Gibbs
Picture research: Todtri Book Publishers

Photo credits: Cover © Rick Vetter; pp. 5, 9, 13, 15, 17, 19, 21 © Elizabeth Myhre;
p. 7 © Pascal Goetgheluck/AUSCAPE; p. 11 © Pascal Goetgheluck/Pho.n.e.

Printed in the United States of America

1 2 3 4 5 6 7 8 9 07 06 05 04 03

**Front cover: Its V-shaped markings make a
hobo spider easy to identify, but its bite is
often mistaken for that of a brown recluse.**

TABLE OF CONTENTS

Words that appear in the glossary are printed in **boldface** type the first time they occur in the text.

HOBO SPIDERS

In the 1970s, emergency room doctors started seeing spider bites that they thought came from a poisonous spider known as the brown recluse. Eventually, they discovered that the bites were from a spider they had not known was dangerous. It was the hobo spider!

People who have been bitten by a hobo spider know how dangerous this creature can be. A hobo spider's **venom**, or poison, can cause a deep wound that takes a long time to heal. Although hobos do not always **inject** venom when they bite, no one should get close enough to take the chance.

Although the results of their bites are the same, a hobo spider is more dangerous than a brown recluse because a hobo is not as shy about biting.

WHAT THEY LOOK LIKE

Hobo spiders have brown bodies and eight long, thin legs. Their bodies, like all spiders' bodies, are divided into two parts: the **cephalothorax** and the **abdomen**. The body of a female hobo spider is about the size of a nickel. The male's body is smaller and narrower, but both males and females have a series of V-shaped marks on their abdomens.

Both male and female hobos also have two short "arms" between their front legs. These arms are called **pedipalps**. On a male hobo, the tips of the pedipalps are very large. They make the spider look as if it is wearing a pair of boxing gloves!

Fine, short hairs cover a hobo spider's body and legs. Its eyes are arranged in two straight rows, with four eyes in each row.

HOW THEY GROW

Each year, in late summer and autumn, male hobo spiders go wandering in search of a mate. This time of year is when hobo spiders are most likely to enter people's houses.

After **mating**, a female hobo lays her eggs, then wraps them in an egg sac made of silk threads, which she produces in her own body. There can be more than a hundred eggs in a single egg sac. Although many other kinds of spiders stay with their eggs and guard them until they hatch, hobo spiders do not. Once the eggs are laid and wrapped, a female hobo finds a safe place for the egg sacs, such as underneath a rock or in a wood pile. Then, she leaves the eggs and never returns.

To provide extra protection for her eggs, this female hobo is covering the egg sac with materials that will help it blend into its surroundings.

The eggs of hobo spiders usually hatch in spring. As the **spiderlings** grow, they go through a process called **molting**. When a spider molts, the hard shell, or **carapace**, covering its body splits open, and the spider crawls out. Then, a new shell hardens around the spider's larger body. Hobo spiderlings molt several times before they are fully grown.

Scientists aren't sure how long hobo spiders live. At first, they thought a hobo's lifetime was only one year. Now, they think that hobo spiders can live up to three years.

When they hatch in spring, the hundreds of tiny white eggs in this egg sac will produce hundreds of hobo spiderlings.

WHERE THEY LIVE

A "hobo" is a homeless person who wanders from place to place. This description could also apply to hobo spiders. These creatures wandered all the way from Europe to North America. The first hobo spiders in North America probably traveled on a cargo ship, arriving some time during the 1920s. They were first identified in 1930, in the port city of Seattle, Washington. Since then, hobo spiders have wandered throughout most of the northwestern United States and into parts of western Canada.

Because they are often seen in houses, and because of their no-nonsense hunting behavior, hobo spiders are also called "**aggressive** house spiders."

Hobo spiders usually live outdoors and are rarely seen. People most often come in contact with the hobos that have wandered indoors.

THEIR WEBS

Hobo spiders are part of the "funnel-web" family. All spiders in this family weave webs shaped like **funnels**. Hobo webs are often found near rocks, plants, or the foundations of houses. The spider lives in the narrow end of the funnel, where it cannot easily be seen.

Hobos, like all funnel-web spiders, spin long silk threads known as trip lines at the openings of their webs. When something touches a trip line, the web shakes. The movement of the web alerts the spider to possible danger — or a tasty snack.

Hobo spiders look for cool, moist places, usually close to the ground, to build their funnel-shaped webs.

HUNTING FOR FOOD

Insects are a hobo spider's favorite food, but capturing them can be a challenge. The sticky webs most spiders spin can easily trap insects, but a hobo's web is dry, so insects do not stick to it.

Hobo spiders have to be fast — and they are! As soon as an insect steps on a trip line, the spider **bolts** out of its web, grabs the insect, and bites it. As it bites, the spider injects the **prey** with venom to kill it. The spider's **fangs** also inject a special juice that liquifies the insect's body tissues so the spider can drink its meal. A hobo spider usually drags its prey to the back of its web before eating.

Even though it has wings, a ladybug that lands on a hobo's trip line is unlikely to escape the spider's quick reaction.

THEIR BITES

All hobo spiders are poisonous — males, females, and even babies — but the male hobo is the most dangerous of all. Not only is the male's poison more powerful than the female's, but, with its wandering habits, an adult male is also more likely to come in contact with people.

Although no one has been known to die from a hobo spider's bite, the venom can do serious damage. The poison attacks body tissues, so the area around a bite might blister or become a deep, open wound. These wounds sometimes takes years to heal and can leave permanent scars.

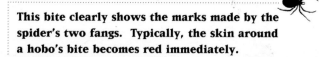

This bite clearly shows the marks made by the spider's two fangs. Typically, the skin around a hobo's bite becomes red immediately.

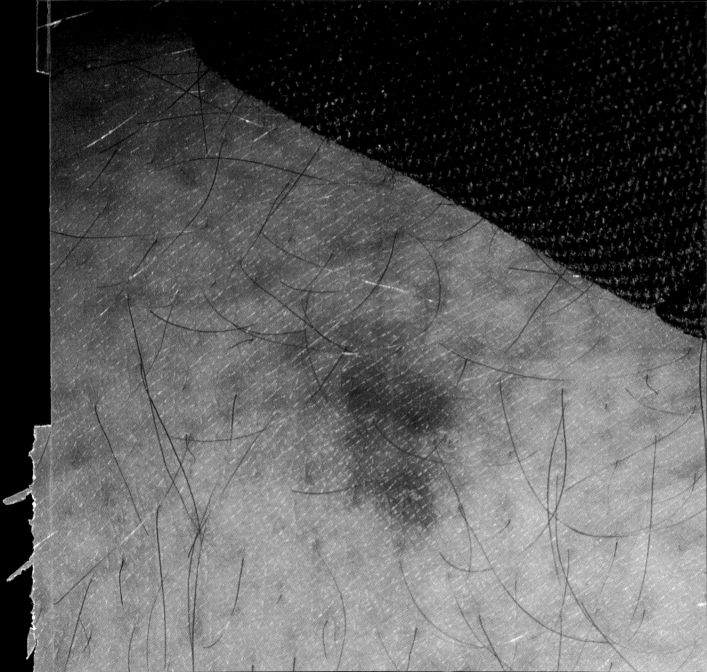

THEIR ENEMIES

Hobo spiders have many enemies, including birds, wasps, praying mantises, house cats, and even other spiders. People, however, are their greatest enemies.

Because of this aggressive spider's poisonous bite, people who find hobos in their houses will do their best to get rid of them. Some people use **insecticide** sprays, but the sprays usually just kill the spiders that prey on hobos. As a result, homes end up with more hobo spiders than they had to begin with. Sticky traps specially designed for hobo spiders are the best way for people to capture and remove them.

This male hobo will probably live longer if it stays outdoors. Its natural lifetime is approximately two years.

MORE TO READ AND VIEW

Books (Nonfiction) *Amazing Spiders*. *Eyewitness Juniors* (series). Alexandra Parsons
  (Random Library)
A House Spider's Life. *Nature Upclose* (series). John Himmelman
  (Children's Press)
I Wonder What It's Like to Be a Spider. Erin M. Hovanec
  (PowerKids Press)
Life Cycle of a Spider. Ron Fridell and Patricia Walsh
  (Heinemann Library)
Spider. *Killer Creatures* (series). David Jefferis and Tony Allan
  (Raintree/Steck-Vaughn)
The Spider. *Life Cycles* (series). Sabrina Crewe (Raintree)
Spiders. *Nature's Wild* (series). Jane Parker Resnick (Rourke)
Spiders Spin Webs. Yvonne Winer (Charlesbridge)

Books (Fiction) *Charlotte's Web*. E. B. White (HarperCollins)
Once I Knew a Spider. Jennifer Owings Dewey (Walker & Co.)
The Spider and the Fly. Mary Botham Howitt (Simon & Schuster)
Spider Weaver: A Legend of Kente. Margaret Musgrove and Julia
  Caims (Scholastic)

Videos (Nonfiction) *Bug City: Spiders & Scorpions*. (Schlessinger Media)
Nightmares of Nature: Spider Attack. (National Geographic)
See How They Grow: Insects & Spiders. (Sony Wonder)

WEB SITES

Web sites change frequently, so one or more of the following recommended sites may no longer be available. To find out more information about hobo spiders, you can also use a good search engine, such as **Yahooligans! [www.yahooligans.com]** or Google [www.google.com]. Here are some keywords to help you: *funnel webs, hobo spiders, poisonous spiders, spider bites, spiders.*

hobospider.org

Most of the Internet agrees that this web site is *the* hobo spider web site. Although it has a lot of information that might be difficult to understand, it is very complete and has some great photographs of both the spider and its web. Don't miss "The Hobo Spider Story" and "Natural History" pages!

arachnophiliac.com/burrow/news/ hobo_attitudes.htm

Hobo spiders make the news! — at least in the northwestern United States. The headline on the "news clipping" in this site is "Hobos Known for Bad Attitudes." The presentation is fun, but the information is factual, complete, and meant to be taken seriously. Don't let the references to cartoons, report cards, and Ozzie and Harriet fool you. They all lead to a vivid (and pretty scary) description of a hobo's bite.

www.hobospider.com

Click on "Spider Info" for some brief but well-organized facts about hobo spiders. Photos of both a male and a female hobo will greet you, along with information about how to identify them. Two other good photos show what a hobo bite (yeech!) looks like and what a funnel web looks like. You can click on links, in several places, for more information, but that information will be harder to read.

www.littleexplorers.com/themes/ spiders.shtml

It is not necessarily about hobo spiders, but this section of *EnchantedLearning.com* has a lot of good information about spiders, and it is a lot of fun, too. Visit this site for spider rhymes and printouts to color and label. Be sure to take the "Spiders Quiz." If you're interested in hobo spiders, you'll really like question #9.

GLOSSARY

You will find these words on the page or pages listed after each definition.
Reading a word in a sentence can help you understand it even better.

abdomen (AB-doh-men) — the back half of a spider's body 6

aggressive (uh-GRES-iv) — bold and forceful, usually the first to start a fight 12, 20

bolts (bohltz) — shoots forward suddenly 16

carapace (KARE-ah-pace) — the hard shell that covers and protects the soft body of an animal and the organs inside it 10

cephalothorax (sef-ah-loh-THOR-acks) — the front half of a spider's body 6

fangs (FANGZ) — long, pointed teeth 16, 18

funnels (FUHN-nuhls) — Y-shaped kitchen utensils used to pour liquids through small openings, such as the neck of a bottle 14

inject (in-JEKT) — to force a liquid into body tissues through a sharp, pointed, needlelike instrument 4, 16

insecticide (in-SEKT-ih-syd) — a chemical manufactured to kill insects and spiders 20

mating (MAYT-ing) — joining with a male to produce young 8

molting (MOHL-ting) — shedding a covering, such as skin, on the outside of the body to make way for new growth 10

pedipalps (PED-ih-palps) — short, armlike attachments that stick out on each side of a spider's mouth 6

prey (PRAY) — (n) an animal that is killed by another animal for food 16; (v) to hunt and kill for food 20

spiderlings (SPY-dur-lingz) — baby spiders 10

venom (VEN-um) — poison that an animal produces in its body and passes into a victim by biting or stinging 4, 16, 18

INDEX